I Can Read GOD'S WORD!

The Lost Sheep

and other stories Jesus told

BARBOUR

PUBLISHING

PHIL A. SMOUSE

In him was life,
and that life was the light of men.

John 1:4 NIV

© 2004 by Phil A. Smouse

ISBN 1-59310-100-7

Published by Barbour Publishing, Inc., P.O. Box 719, Uhrichsville, Ohio 44683
www.barbourbooks.com

Our mission is to publish and distribute inspirational products offering exceptional value and biblical encouragement to the masses.

 Member of the
Evangelical Christian
Publishers Association

Printed in China.
5 4 3

CONTENTS

A NOTE TO PARENTS. . .

I Can Read God's Word! is a simple idea
with a simple goal: to put the Word
of God on the lips of God's children.

I've drawn from the practical teachings
of Jesus in the New Testament and the
promises of God in the Old and "translated"
them into an easy-to-read paraphrase that
is absolutely faithful to the original text
while staying as close as possible to the
phonics-based reading curriculum your
children are learning at home or in school.

Twenty-three long years went by before I ever read a single page of the Bible for myself. But if God answers prayer (and you know He does), before *this* year is over you will hear a familiar little voice say, "Mom, Dad, listen. . .*I Can Read God's Word!*"

Enjoy!

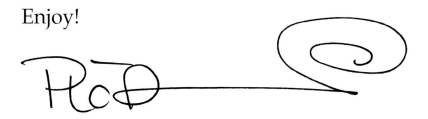

Phil A. Smouse

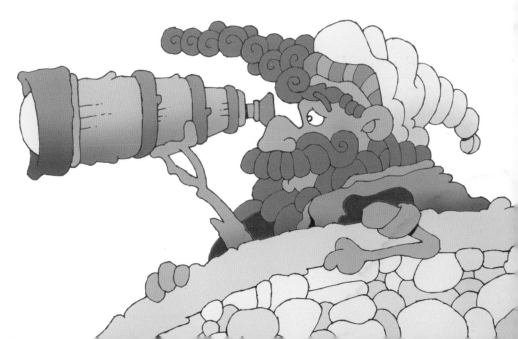

THE LOST SHEEP

Matthew 18:12-13

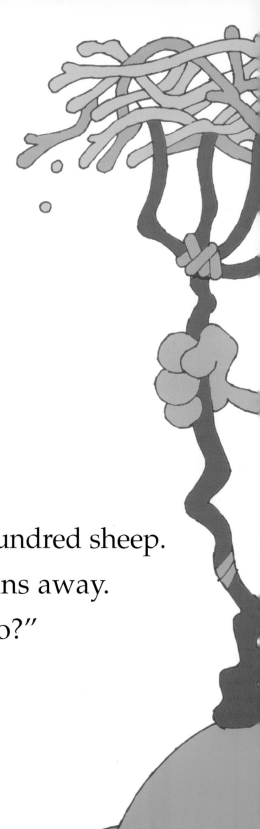

Jesus said,
"A man has a hundred sheep.
One of them runs away.
What will he do?"

"Will he leave
all the other sheep?
Will he go to find
the one that is lost?"

"He will!"

"But when he
finds the lost sheep
what will he do?"

"No. He will shout for joy!"

"His little sheep was lost.
Now she is safe in his
arms again."

THE SEED AND THE SOWER

Matthew 13:3-8

Jesus said,
"A farmer went out
to plant his seed."

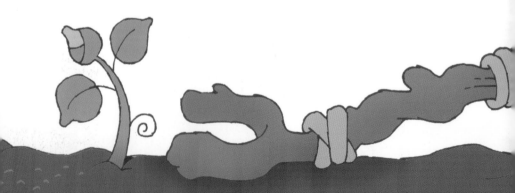

"As he spread the seed some fell on a path."

"But a bird ate it all up!"

"Some fell on rocky ground."

"The soil was not very deep.
The plants grew quickly. "

"But their roots were weak.
When the sun came up
the plants dried up in the heat."

"Some seed fell in the weeds."

"But the weeds
choked the tiny
plants. Soon
they all died."

"But some seed fell on good ground.

And those plants grew,

and grew,"

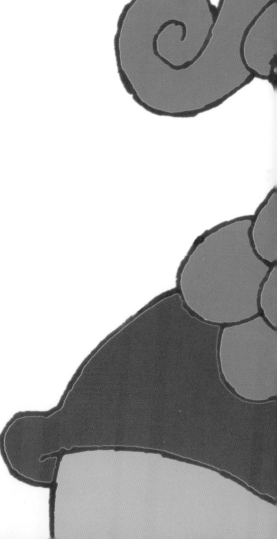

"And GREW!

And they gave the farmer
a big crop. There were thirty. . .
sixty. . .even one hundred
times more than he had
planted!"

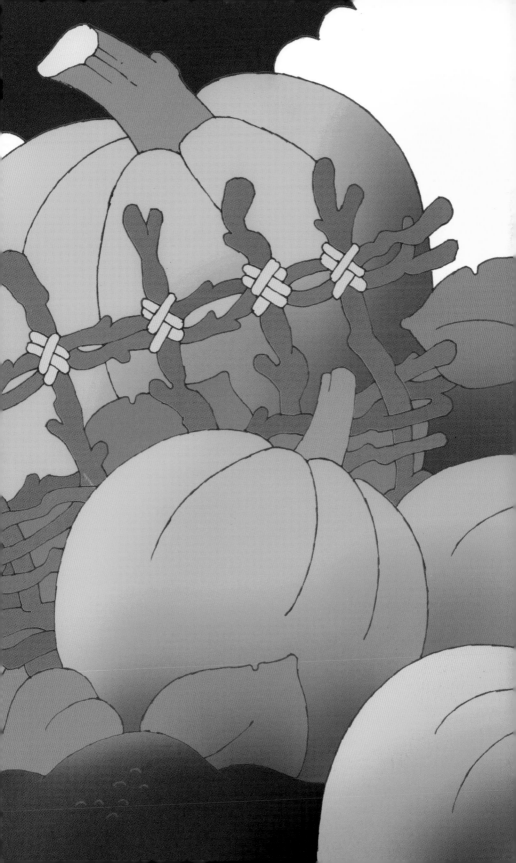

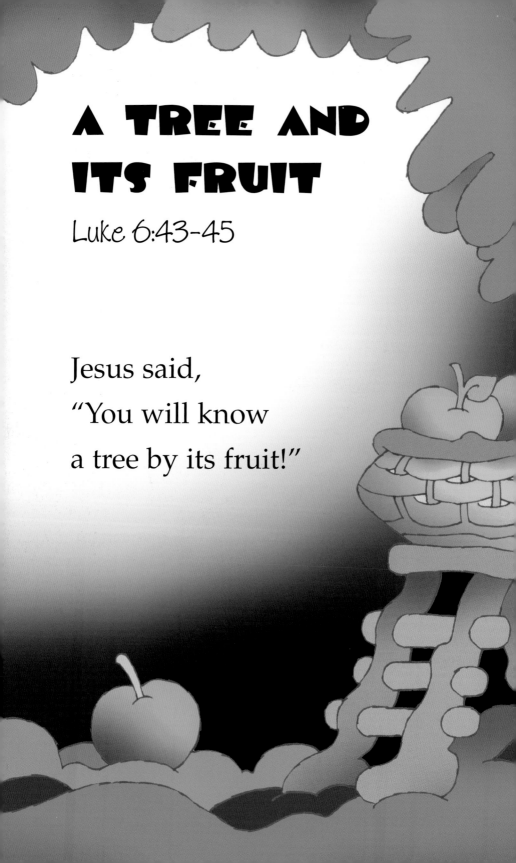

A TREE AND ITS FRUIT

Luke 6:43-45

Jesus said,
"You will know
a tree by its fruit!"

"A good tree does not grow bad fruit."

"And a bad tree
does not grow
good fruit!"

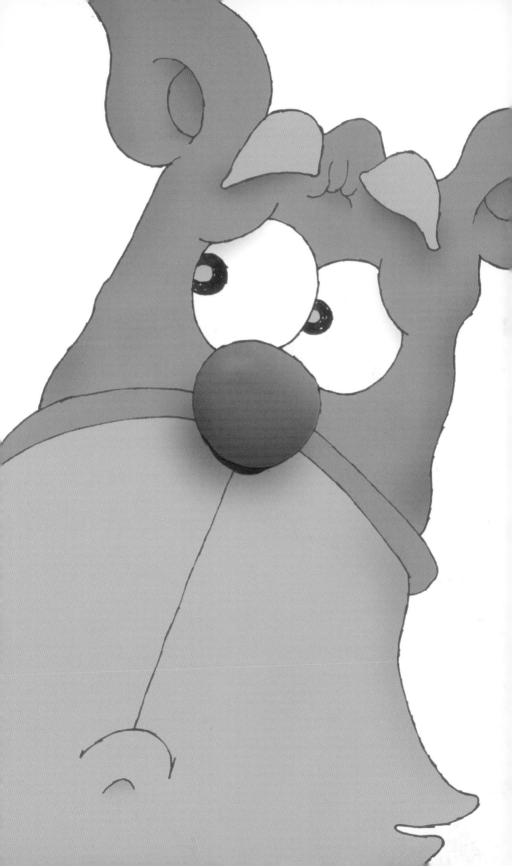

"Can you pick apples from a thornbush?"

"Of course not!"

"So remember this.
A good man does
good things because
his heart is good."

"An evil man does
bad things because
his heart is evil."

"What kind of fruit
is in *your* heart?"

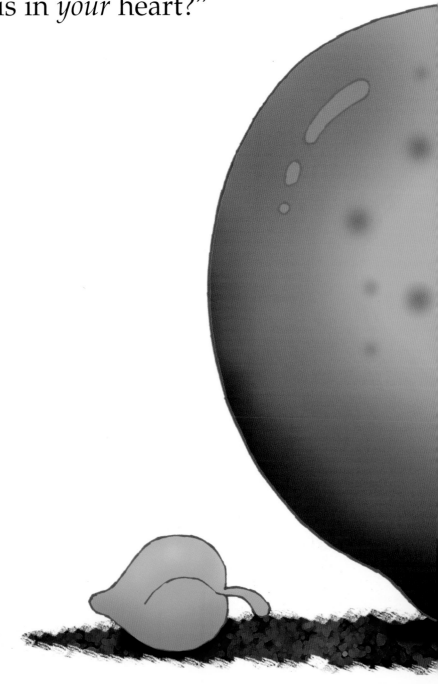

LOOK UP!

Matthew 6:25-26

Jesus said,
"Do not worry
about the things
you need."

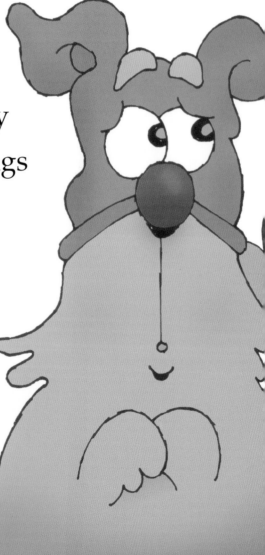

"You will always have good food to eat."

"You will always have
warm clothes to wear."

"Look up!"

"They do not work."

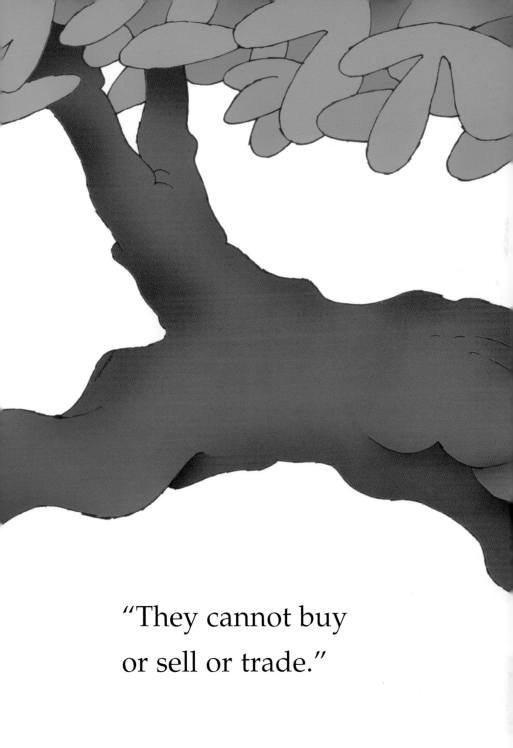

"They cannot buy
or sell or trade."

"And they have
no place to put anything
even if they could."

"But God feeds them.
He cares for them
just the same."

"So why do you worry?"

"God loves you more than anything else in the world!"

THE LOST SHEEP
Matthew 18:12–13

"If a man has a hundred sheep, and one of them goes astray, does he not leave the ninety-nine and go to the mountains to seek the one that is straying? And if he should find it, assuredly, I say to you, he rejoices more over that sheep than over the ninety-nine that did not go astray."

THE SEED AND THE SOWER
Matthew 13:3–8

"Behold, a sower went out to sow. And as he sowed, some seed fell by the wayside; and the birds came and devoured them. Some fell on stony places, where they did not have much earth; and they immediately sprang up because they had no depth of earth. But when the sun was up they were scorched, and because they had no root they withered away. And some fell among thorns, and the thorns sprang up and choked them. But others fell on good ground and yielded a crop: some a hundredfold, some sixty, some thirty."

A TREE AND ITS FRUIT
Luke 6:43–45

"A good tree does not bear bad fruit, nor does a bad tree bear good fruit. For every tree is known by its own fruit. For men do not gather figs from thorns, nor do they gather grapes from a bramble bush. A good man out of the good treasure of his heart brings forth good; and an evil man out of the evil treasure of his heart brings forth evil. For out of the abundance of the heart his mouth speaks."

LOOK UP!
Matthew 6:25–26

"Do not worry about your life, what you will eat or what you will drink; nor about your body, what you will put on. Is not life more than food and the body more than clothing? Look at the birds of the air, for they neither sow nor reap nor gather into barns; yet your heavenly Father feeds them. Are you not of more value than they?"